FAMILY ★★ STAND

FOOTBALL CLUB
READY

RANGERS

EXIT 5

EXIT 5

PILLAR BOX RED

in association with

MATCH! & WorldSoccer

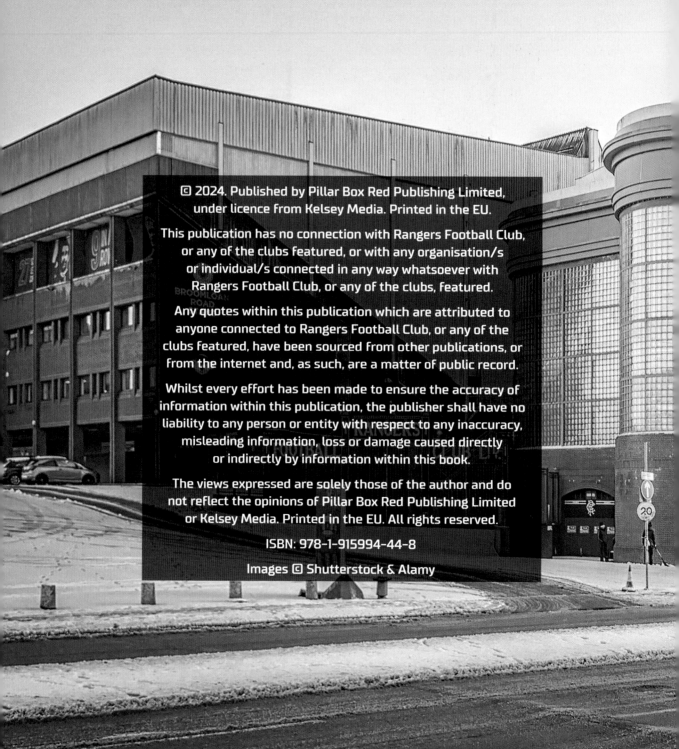

# RANGERS 2025

Written by
Iain Williamson

Designed by
Jon Dalrymple

AN INDEPENDENT PRODUCTION

# CONTENTS

# SEASON

Season 2023-24 brought some success for Rangers as they recaptured the League Cup for the first time in 13 years, but only after a change of manager. Ultimately, bad luck with injuries, a failure to beat arch-rivals Celtic, and an inability to close out the season with the treble in reach, made it a frustrating year for the Ibrox faithful. Take a look at how the season unfolded in rollercoaster style.

## AUGUST 2023

Optimism was high after some big-money purchases in the summer but defeat at Kilmarnock on opening day got Rangers' season off to a shocking start.

Wins over Livingston and Ross County got the league campaign back on-track but after squeezing past Servette of Switzerland, Rangers were unable to repeat last season's victory over PSV Eindhoven and crashed out of the Champions League before the group stage.

### MEGA MOMENT

Summer signings Sam Lammers, Danilo, Abdallah Sima and Keiran Dowell notched all the goals in a 4-0 romp over Livingston at Ibrox but the big-money buys were unable to help secure Champions League qualification.

### STAR MAN

Captain James Tavernier showed the new boys how it is done with a hot start in front of goal. His four goals in August set him up to be the club's top-scorer once again, with a total of 24 goals bagged by the end of the season.

| DATE | COMP | HOME | RESULT | AWAY |
|------|------|------|--------|------|
| 05/08 | SPFL | Kilmarnock | 1-0 | Rangers |
| 09/08 | UCL | Rangers | 2-1 | Servette |
| 12/08 | SPFL | Rangers | 4-0 | Livingston |
| 15/08 | UCL | Servette | 1-1 | Rangers |
| 19/08 | SLC | Rangers | 2-1 | Greenock Morton |
| 22/08 | UCL | Rangers | 2-2 | PSV |
| 26/08 | SPFL | Ross County | 0-2 | Rangers |
| 30/08 | UCL | PSV | 5-1 | Rangers |

# REVIEW

## SEPTEMBER 2023

September was book-ended by home defeats to Celtic and Aberdeen and saw Rangers fall 7 points behind their main rivals by the end of the month. These poor performances plus fan dissatisfaction and a Champions League exit combined to cost manager Michael Beale his job just two months into the season.

Positivity was thin on the ground but a home win over Real Betis was a good start in the Europa League and another 4-0 thumping of Livingston ensured progress to the League Cup semi-finals.

## MEGA MOMENT

A close-range poke in from Abdallah Sima against Betis crowned a lively European night at Ibrox. The first of Sima's three goals in September secured a win that would turn out to be crucial by the end of the group stage.

## STAR MAN

Goalkeeper Jack Butland kept 4 clean sheets in 6 games during September. A summer signing from Crystal Palace, England international Butland quickly established himself as Rangers No. 1 and at the end of a fine season, he was voted the club's Player of the Year by both team-mates and supporters.

| DATE | COMP | HOME | RESULT | AWAY |
|------|------|------|--------|------|
| 03/09 | SPFL | Rangers | 0-1 | Celtic |
| 16/09 | SPFL | St Johnstone | 0-2 | Rangers |
| 21/09 | UEL | Rangers | 1-0 | Real Betis |
| 24/09 | SPFL | Rangers | 1-0 | Motherwell |
| 27/09 | SLC | Rangers | 4-0 | Livingston |
| 30/09 | SPFL | Rangers | 1-3 | Aberdeen |

# SEASON

## OCTOBER 2023

With Steven Davis in interim charge, Rangers' woes continued with a disappointing defeat in Cyprus. A convincing 3-0 win in Paisley was an excellent response, as James Tavernier helped send the club into the international break on a high with goals from a penalty and a free-kick.

After the International Break, the Philippe Clement era began with a hugely encouraging 4-goal win over Hibs at Ibrox, followed by a battling draw in Prague and an astonishing recovery against Hearts to preserve the new manager's unbeaten record.

## MEGA MOMENT

Philippe Clement's honeymoon period as manager looked to be coming to a premature end against Hearts in only his 2nd home game in charge, before a 90th minute Tavernier penalty and an even later winner from a masked Danilo stole the points back for the Ibrox club.

## STAR MAN

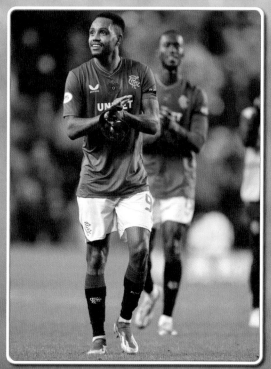

Starting at the end of September, Abdallah Sima scored in 5 consecutive matches (under 3 different managers), culminating in a double against Hibs in Clement's First game. The Brighton loanee's form earned him the Premiership Player of the Month award for October.

| DATE | COMP | HOME | RESULT | AWAY |
|------|------|------|--------|------|
| 05/10 | UEL | Aris Limassol | 2-1 | Rangers |
| 08/10 | SPFL | St Mirren | 0-3 | Rangers |
| 21/10 | SPFL | Rangers | 4-0 | Hibernian |
| 26/10 | UEL | Sparta Prague | 0-0 | Rangers |
| 29/10 | SPFL | Rangers | 2-1 | Hearts |

# REVIEW

## NOVEMBER 2023

An unbeaten month went some way to restoring confidence and pride after a dodgy start to the season. A 5-goal rout of Dundee was the prequel to Clement's first Hampden appearance in the League Cup semi-final against Hearts, who were despatched comfortably.

Wins over Livingston and Sparta Prague kept up the momentum, but it took a very late Tavernier penalty to salvage a draw at Pittodrie and a first Rangers goal for Ross McCausland to keep Europa League hopes alive at home to Aris.

## STAR MAN

A trademark 'Tavernier Double' of a free kick and a penalty helped fire Rangers to Hampden glory against Hearts. In all, he scored 5 goals in November, comprising of 1 free kick and 4 penalties. He even had the luxury of missing his first penalty of the game against Livingston before redeeming himself with a successful spot kick later in the game.

## MEGA MOMENT

A devastating opening 20 minutes against Sparta brought a raucous Ibrox to its feet. Danilo created his own chance by robbing a defender before slotting home and Todd Cantwell's first goal of the season was another delightful finish. Rangers had to hold off a late Sparta comeback but secured the points they needed to grab 2nd place in the group.

| DATE | COMP | HOME | RESULT | AWAY |
|---|---|---|---|---|
| 01/11 | SPFL | Dundee | 0-5 | Rangers |
| 05/11 | SLC | Hearts | 1-3 | Rangers |
| 09/11 | UEL | Rangers | 2-1 | Sparta Prague |
| 12/11 | SPFL | Livingston | 0-2 | Rangers |
| 26/11 | SPFL | Aberdeen | 1-1 | Rangers |
| 30/11 | UEL | Rangers | 1-1 | Aris Limassol |

# SEASON

## DECEMBER 2023

A busy and successful month saw the club progress from their Europa League group after beating Betis on a triumphant return to Seville. The club also picked up some silverware, lifting the Viaplay / Scottish League Cup for the first time since 2011 with a 1-0 Hampden win over Aberdeen.

A further 5 wins in the league reduced the gap to leaders Celtic to just 2 points before defeat in the Old Firm derby brought the year to a disappointing end.

Winners 2023/

## MEGA MOMENT

A couple of weeks after his goal won the League Cup Final, James Tavernier's sensational 'top bins' free kick on 88 minutes brought late drama to the last Old Firm game of the year, although Rangers were not able to grab an equaliser despite a frantic end to the game.

## STAR MAN

Abdallah Sima scored match-winning goals in the first two games of the month. The Senegal international also netted in the following games against Dundee and Real Betis to complete a sensational 4-game burst at the start of December.

| DATE | COMP | HOME | RESULT | AWAY |
|------|------|------|--------|------|
| 03/12 | SPFL | Rangers | 2-0 | St Mirren |
| 06/12 | SPFL | Hearts | 0-1 | Rangers |
| 09/12 | SPFL | Rangers | 3-1 | Dundee |
| 14/12 | UEL | Real Betis | 2-3 | Rangers |
| 17/12 | SLC | Rangers | 1-0 | Aberdeen |
| 20/12 | SPFL | Rangers | 2-0 | St Johnstone |
| 24/12 | SPFL | Motherwell | 0-2 | Rangers |
| 30/12 | SPFL | Celtic | 2-1 | Rangers |

# REVIEW

## JANUARY 2024

In a month interrupted by the winter break, Rangers won all 4 of their competitive games to surge up the table and progress in the cup.

Summer recruits Sam Lammers and Jose Cifuentes both left the club on loan in the transfer window, while Rangers also lost Abdallah Sima to an injury sustained on AFCON duty with Senegal.

Mohamed Diomande and loan signings Fabio Silva (Wolves) and Oscar Cortes (Lens) came in as Clement began to reshape his squad.

## MEGA MOMENT

Cyriel Dessers scored the only goal of the game in Paisley to complete a short unbeaten month for the Ibrox men. That goal was the Nigerian international striker's 3rd in consecutive games as he stepped up his scoring form in the absence of Danilo and Sima through injury.

## STAR MAN

Rangers' resurgence under Philippe Clement saw him recognised with his first SPFL Premiership Manager of the Month award. Rangers scored 11 goals and conceded only 2 in January as the new manager's impact became clear.

| DATE | COMP | HOME | RESULT | AWAY |
|------|------|------|--------|------|
| 02/01 | SPFL | Rangers | 3-1 | Kilmarnock |
| 20/01 | SC | Dumbarton | 1-4 | Rangers |
| 24/01 | SPFL | Hibernian | 0-3 | Rangers |
| 27/01 | SPFL | St Mirren | 0-1 | Rangers |

# SEASON

## FEBRUARY 2024

A busy February saw another unbeaten month as Rangers went top of the league for the first time since August 2022.

4 clean sheets and only 3 goals conceded were a key element as John Souttar and Connor Goldson formed an impressive partnership in front of Jack Butland.

Rangers also scored 20 goals in the month, with Dessers, Tavernier and Silva leading the way, but the rest of the goals were shared between 10 different players.

## MEGA MOMENT

A thumping 5-0 win over Hearts at Ibrox was a significant statement and consolidated Rangers' narrow lead in the Premiership chase.

Cyriel Dessers bagged his 3rd and 4th goals of the month with the scoring completed by a trio of winter recruits as Diomande, Cortes and Silva all netted.

## STAR MAN

Philippe Clement earned his second consecutive Manager of the Month award after his team's unbeaten run since the turn of the year vaulted them to the top of the Premiership. With the Winter signings contributing well, Clement credited his success to a team effort including the coaching staff and players.

| DATE | COMP | HOME | RESULT | AWAY |
|------|------|------|--------|------|
| 03/02 | SPFL | Rangers | 3-0 | Livingston |
| 06/02 | SPFL | Rangers | 2-1 | Aberdeen |
| 10/02 | SC | Rangers | 2-0 | Ayr United |
| 14/02 | SPFL | Rangers | 3-1 | Ross County |
| 18/02 | SPFL | St Johnstone | 0-3 | Rangers |
| 24/02 | SPFL | Rangers | 5-0 | Hearts |
| 28/02 | SPFL | Kilmarnock | 1-2 | Rangers |

# REVIEW

## MARCH 2024

Rangers' 2-month unbeaten run crashed to a halt on the second day of March as Motherwell plundered the points with their first league win at Ibrox since 1997.

A great effort against Benfica in Lisbon was undone by a penalty and a Goldson own goal, before a single goal conceded on a rainy Govan night saw Rangers eliminated from European competition.

Two wins over Hibs saw the club make progress in the Scottish Cup and league, however Rangers only played one match in the second part of the month due to an international break and the controversial postponement of the game at Dens Park, Dundee due to a waterlogged pitch.

## MEGA MOMENT

A pulsating Scottish Cup quarter-final tie at Easter Road saw Rangers triumph over 9-man Hibs after a tempestuous battle. John Lundstram showed great desire to bundle home the rebound from a blocked Tavernier penalty before Daniel Silva sent his team through with a delightful jink and finish, which he gleefully celebrated while sitting on the perimeter wall in front of the fans.

## STAR MAN

David Marshall of Hibs saved two James Tavernier penalties in March, but the Englishman's precision low drive in the league game at Ibrox made the skipper the highest scoring defender in British football history.

| DATE | COMP | HOME | RESULT | AWAY |
|------|------|------|--------|------|
| 02/03 | SPFL | Rangers | 1-2 | Motherwell |
| 07/03 | UEL | Benfica | 2-2 | Rangers |
| 10/03 | SC | Hibernian | 0-2 | Rangers |
| 14/03 | UEL | Rangers | 0-1 | Benfica |
| 30/03 | SPFL | Rangers | 3-1 | Hibernian |

# SEASON

## APRIL 2024

Rangers went into the penultimate month of the season with a domestic treble seemingly within their grasp. They battled hard to win a point at home to Celtic but a shock first-ever defeat to Ross County and a disappointing draw in the twice-postponed game at Dundee handed the initiative back to their Glasgow rivals.

A Scottish Cup semi-final win continued Rangers' record of never having lost to Hearts at Hampden and set up a season-ending Old Firm Final.

## MEGA MOMENT

Rabbi Matondo's stunning 93rd minute equaliser against Celtic capped a second comeback from Rangers and sealed a vital point from the crunch clash. The Welshman's long-range effort was later voted as Goal of the Season at the PFA Scotland Awards.

## STAR MAN

Whilst not generally regarded as a lethal finisher, Cyriel Dessers' industry and skill bagged him another two vital goals in the Scottish Cup semi-final, both assisted by Todd Cantwell. Dessers flourished after the arrival of Philippe Clement and would go on to score 22 goals over the season.

| DATE | COMP | HOME | RESULT | AWAY |
|------|------|------|--------|------|
| 07/04 | SPFL | Rangers | 3-3 | Celtic |
| 14/04 | SPFL | Ross County | 3-2 | Rangers |
| 17/04 | SPFL | Dundee | 0-0 | Rangers |
| 21/04 | SC | Rangers | 2-0 | Hearts |
| 28/04 | SPFL | St Mirren | 1-2 | Rangers |

# REVIEW

## MAY 2024

Rangers did their best to put post-split pressure on Celtic with big wins over Kilmarnock and Dundee, but it was not to be. A third Old Firm league defeat of the season effectively delivered a 54th title to Celtic Park and Clement and his team will need to regroup and strengthen for another massive challenge in 2024/25.

In the Scottish Cup final, it looked like Rangers had finally got the better of Celtic when the returning Abdallah Sima bundled over the line in the 60th minute but the 'goal' was ruled out for a push, before Adam Idah ensured it would be green ribbons on the cup with a 90th minute tap-in.

## MEGA MOMENT

The deciding Old Firm game on 11th of May started to go wrong when Celtic scored in the 35th minute. Within minutes, the normally dependable John Lundstram had deflected the ball past Jack Butland for an own goal and a red card for a reckless challenge before half-time was a sad end to his Rangers career. That crazy spell also included a goal back through Cyriel Dessers but it effectively ended Rangers' title hopes.

| DATE | COMP | HOME | RESULT | AWAY |
|------|------|------|--------|------|
| 05/05 | SPFL | Rangers | 4-1 | Kilmarnock |
| 11/05 | SPFL | Celtic | 2-1 | Rangers |
| 14/05 | SPFL | Rangers | 5-2 | Dundee |
| 18/05 | SPFL | Hearts | 3-3 | Rangers |
| 25/05 | SC | Celtic | 1-0 | Rangers |

## STAR MAN

With injuries continuing to pile up, Clement relied upon good performances from the likes of Scott Wright, Ben Davies, Ross McCausland and Tom Lawrence in May, but Dujon Sterling's emergence as an essential and versatile performer all over the park made him indispensable in the run-in.

# '10 MOHAMED DIOMANDE FACTS!

**1** Mohamed Baba Diomande was born on 30th October 2001 in the Abidjan suburb of Yopougon, Ivory Coast.

**2** The young Diomande trained in Ghana for seven years at the prestigious Right to Dream Academy. Other Academy graduates include Mohammed Kudus of West Ham and AZ Alkmaar star, Ibrahim Sadiq.

**3** As a teenager, Diomande's skills earned him a move to professional football in Denmark. He made his debut for Danish Superliga club, FC Nordsjaelland, on 19th February 2020 against AC Horsens.

**4** Diomande went on to make 111 appearances for Nordsjaelland, registering 13 goals and 14 assists, including a notable performance against Fenerbahce in the UEFA Conference League in November 2023.

**5** On 26th January 2024, Diomande signed for Rangers, initially on a loan deal but with an obligation to buy for a fee of around £4.3m. He made his debut for the club on 6th February 2024, at home to Aberdeen.

**6** Diomande's first goal for Rangers was a stunning long-range strike to open the scoring at St Johnstone on 18th February 2024.

**7** His first goal in front of the fans at Ibrox came one week later, scoring in the 2nd minute against Hearts to start a 5-0 rout.

**8** A broken thumb sustained in the Old Firm 3-3 draw in April 2024 restricted Diomande to 19 appearances in his first half season at Rangers, but that was enough to make a big impression on Rangers fans.

**9** The loan move became permanent in the summer of 2024, with the player contracted at Ibrox until 2028 and expected to play an important role in midfield.

**10** In 2024, Diomande declared his allegiance to the Ivory Coast international team, rejecting an approach from Ghana, for whom he was also eligible. He won his first full cap for Les Elephants on 7 June 2024 in a World Cup qualifier at home to Gabon.

# LOVE MATCH?
## GET IT DELIVERED EVERY FORTNIGHT!

**SAVING 57% ON THE FULL SHOP PRICE!* ONLY £39.99 FOR 13 ISSUES!**

## PACKED EVERY ISSUE WITH...

★ Red-hot gear

★ News & gossip

★ Stats & quizzes

★ Massive stars

★ Posters & pics

& loads more!

# LEAGUE CUP MOMENTS

## No.1 2023/24

## THE DETAILS

Rangers' triumph in the 2023/24 League Cup Final was the 28th time they had lifted this trophy – by far the highest winning total, ahead of Celtic on 21 wins. Rangers were the inaugural winners when the competition was launched in season 1946/47. Since then, Rangers have won the cup a remarkable 36% of the time, so on average they win this cup every three years. Having last won it in 2010/11, that 12-season gap is the joint longest in the club's history, alongside a similarly barren run in the 1950s.

| RANGERS 1 | ABERDEEN 0 |
|---|---|
| Tavernier 76 | – |
| Hampden Park 17th December 2024 ||

FIR
FO

# ST TROPHY CLEMENT

## THE STORY

Just two months after starting his new job, Philippe Clement masterminded the first trophy win of his Ibrox career and ensured that European qualification for his club was secured before Christmas. In truth, this was a scrappy, attritional game as Rangers struggled to break down the well-organised system of 6-times winners Aberdeen, but the result was all that mattered. The only goal of the game came from a deep Borna Barisic cross which was fired home at the back post by Rangers' captain James Tavernier. It was fitting that the skipper stole the show again as it was his two goals that clinched a semi-final win over Hearts and his League Cup medal completed a personal career domestic treble for the prolific Englishman.

# PHILIPPE CLEMENT SCRAPBOOK

Philippe Clement was appointed as the 19th manager of Rangers in October 2023 and subsequently re-committed to the Ibrox cause until 2028 before the start of this season. Here are some interesting facts about the boss.

## CLEVER CLOGS

The son of two school-teacher parents, Philippe may be the most highly-qualified manager in football.

He initially studied at The Royal Atheneum of Antwerp before earning a Law Degree at the University of Antwerp. Combining studies with a playing career, he added a Masters in Law and a postgraduate diploma in Sports Management. Philippe is also fluent in four languages; Dutch, English, French and German.

## SENT TO COVENTRY

After success as a player in Belgium with Beerschot and Genk, Clement joined Coventry City for season 1998/99, playing alongside club captain Gary McAllister for manager Gordon Strachan, who famously helped out as a baby-sitter for Clement's young family. A broken cheekbone in pre-season and a subsequent back injury restricted Philippe to 16 appearances in the Midlands.

## BELGIUM

Clement made his international debut against Norway in March 1998. He was selected for the 1998 World Cup finals and Euro 2000. His only international goal came in Bulgaria in June 2003 and his final caps were gained in 2007.

## CLUB BRUGGE

After Coventry, Clement spent the next 10 seasons playing for Club Brugge back in Belgium, making 326 appearances. From 2012/13, he was part of the management team at Brugge during a very successful period for the club. After two stints as interim manager, Clement moved on in 2017 to become head coach at Waasland-Beveren and then another former club Genk, where he won the league in 2018/19. That earned him a return to Brugge as the boss and two more titles followed.

## MONACO TO GOVAN

After a short period as head coach of AS Monaco, Clement was ousted and ultimately swapped a relatively idyllic Monegasque lifestyle for the sometimes-toxic goldfish bowl of Glasgow.

The Clement era got off to a red-hot start as a rejuvenated Rangers team went unbeaten in his first 16 games as Light Blues boss, lifting the League Cup and two Manager of the Month awards along the way.

Unfortunately, the honeymoon period came to a jolting end as Rangers came up just short in both league and cup. Clement will now be well aware that the success of his time at Ibrox will ultimately be determined by performances against Celtic and trophies won.

## THE SUPPORT TEAM

Philippe was joined in Glasgow by former Club Brugge colleague Stephan Van Der Heyden, who was appointed as assistant manager.

Like Clement, Van Der Heyden played for Club Brugge and Belgium, winning 4 caps. In an itinerant career, he also played outside of Belgium for Roda JC (Netherlands), Lille (France) and South Melbourne (Australia). After retiring as a player, he has served as assistant manager at Sporting Lokeren and Club Brugge in his homeland, Vardar Skopje in North Macedonia, the national team of Jordan and Kerala Blasters in India.

## FACT FILE

**Date of Birth:**
22 March 1974

**Place of Birth:**
Antwerp, Belgium

**Height:**
6 ft 3 in

**International Caps:**
38 appearances for Belgium

**Playing position:**
Centre back/defensive midfielder

# SPOT THE DIFFERENCE

On 19th August, 2023, Rangers played Greenock Morton at Ibrox Stadium in the second round tie of the Viaplay Cup qualifiers. Can you spot the 10 differences between these two photos of the match? Answers on page 61.

# CAN YOU RECOGNISE THIS TOP PLAYER?

Answer on page 61.

# WHO AM I?

Answer on page 61.

## CLUES

**1** I was born in Belgium

**2** I was the joint top scorer in the Netherlands' Eredivisie in 2019/20

**3** I played for Cremonese in Italy's Serie A

**4** I made my debut for Nigeria in October 2020

**5** In 2023/24, I scored for Rangers in all five competitions; Scottish Premiership, Scottish Cup, League Cup, Champions League and Europa League

# EUROPEAN NIGHTS

Starting with their very first European Cup fixture against Nice in 1956/57, continental adventures have been a highlight of virtually every Rangers season since. The club have enjoyed considerable success, reaching five finals over the years and winning the European Cup Winner's Cup in 1972.

The 2023/24 campaign once again featured several raucous European nights at Ibrox and some battling overseas performances, before ultimately ending with another heart-breaking exit.

## UEFA CHAMPIONS LEAGUE

### 3rd Qualifying Round

Rangers 3-2 Servette (Aggregate)

Rangers entered UEFA's flagship competition in early August with a 3rd qualifying round tie against Servette of Switzerland. A slender 2-1 Ibrox lead was cancelled out in a sweltering first half in Geneva before James Tavernier's second goal of the tie secured qualification.

### Play-Off Round

Rangers 3-7 PSV Eindhoven (Aggregate)

Paired at this stage for the 2nd season in a row, Rangers were again held to a 2-2 draw against PSV at Ibrox. This time there was to be no repeat of the previous year's victory in The Netherlands as the Gers crashed to a heavy 5-1 defeat, with Connor Goldson's own goal a particular low-light.

## UEFA Europa League Group Stage

Rangers got points on the board early with an opening night victory over Real Betis in front of another big, loud European crowd at Ibrox. A tame losing performance in Cyprus under caretaker manager Steven Davis undermined that good work though, as all four teams finished Matchday 2 on 3 points.

The Light Blues came back from a tricky trip to Prague with a goal-less draw thanks to a fine show by Jack Butland in goals. In the reverse fixture, the fans roared Rangers on to a 2-1-win courtesy of goals by Cantwell and Danilo.

Rangers were frustrated once again by Aris Limassol, this time at Ibrox, relying on a 2nd half Ross McCausland equaliser to snatch a draw. That left them needing a big result from a return trip to the Andalusian city of Seville and that is exactly what the team delivered, with a battling performance and a late Kemar Roofe winner sending them through as group winners.

## Round of 16

### Benfica 3-2 Rangers

Rangers shocked 2-time European champions Benfica in Lisbon by twice taking the lead at Estadio da Luz. A brave effort was undone by a contentious penalty and another bizarre own goal by Connor Goldson – his second of this European campaign and his 3rd overall in Europa League matches.

Rangers again took the fight to Benfica on a wet and noisy night at Ibrox in March. The home crowd were silenced by a breakaway goal from Rafa Silva in the second half and despite a spirited effort, that was enough to bring Rangers' European odyssey to an end for another year.

# RANGERS WOMEN

## 2023/24 SEASON REVIEW

Under new manager Jo Potter, the women's team took a big step forward in 2023/24, capturing both domestic cups and coming within minutes of winning a sensational treble in a dramatic finale to an enthralling season.

The presence of former England Lioness Potter in the technical area helped attract several star players from south of the Border in advance of the season. Experienced Welsh international Rachel Rowe joined from Reading and went on to win the SWPL Player of the Year award after a stellar season in midfield.

Rio Hardy was another important signing. The former Durham Women striker went on to finish as the club's top-scorer with 34 goals in her first season.

Rangers' season got off to a terrific start with an unbeaten run which only ended with a narrow defeat to Celtic Women in March. Kirsty Howat won SWPL Player of the Month honours in both September and October after a sparkling spell in front of goal, including 4 goals against Hibs in a 7-0 win at Ibrox. Kirsty also finished the league season strongly with 5 goals in the crucial last week, victimising Hibs again with a hat-trick in the penultimate game.

Rangers retained the SWPL Cup in March but faltered slightly in the league after two successive draws in February and a narrow defeat in the Old Firm game. A second defeat, at Hearts in April, allowed Celtic to snatch top spot in the league but a Scottish Cup semi-final victory over their arch-rivals kept Rangers' treble hopes alive going into the last month of the season.

By the time Rangers welcomed Celtic to Broadwood in early May, they were back level on points but with a significant goal difference deficit. Needing a win, Rangers were frustrated by a goalless draw after Mia McAulay's fine late strike struck the crossbar. The Light Blues maintained their challenge on the last day of the season with a 4-0 victory over Partick Thistle. For 89 minutes, that looked like it might be enough as Hibs fought for a draw at Celtic Park, before Amy Gallacher's late strike clinched Celtic's first SWPL title.

Rangers completed an outstanding season by winning the Women's Scottish Cup for the first time ever, beating Hearts 2-0 in the final. After collecting 2 out of 3 domestic trophies and clinching a Champions League return, Potter will be looking to achieve even greater success in 2024/25.

# RANGERS WOMEN CUP DOUBLE

Rangers Women clinched their first trophy of the Potter era with a commanding 4-1 victory over Partick Thistle to retain the trophy in front of a record attendance of 4,786.

Young Mia McAulay opened the scoring on her way to a Player of the Match performance and further strikes by summer signings Rachel Rowe and Rio Hardy put Rangers in control before half-time. Liv McLoughlin added another just after the break as Potter's side eased to a comfortable win.

## SCOTTISH WOMEN'S PREMIER LEAGUE CUP FINAL

**WHEN:** 24 MARCH 2024
**WHERE:** TYNECASTLE PARK, EDINBURGH
**SCORE:** RANGERS 4
**WHO:** McAulay 13, Rowe 35, Hardy 47, McLoughlin 53
**SCORE:** PARTICK THISTLE 1
**WHO:** Donaldson 18

|  | HOME | RESULT | AWAY |
|---|---|---|---|
| R2 | Hearts | 1-4 | Rangers |
| QF | Rangers | 7-0 | Boroughmuir Thistle |
| SF | Celtic | 2-3 | Rangers |

# ROUTE TO THE FINAL

## WOMEN'S SCOTTISH CUP FINAL

**WHEN:** 26 MAY 2024
**WHERE:** HAMPDEN PARK, GLASGOW
**SCORE:** RANGERS 2
**WHO:** McLoughlin 24, Arnot 86
**SCORE:** HEARTS 0

After finishing runners-up three times previously, Rangers won the Scottish Cup for the first time with a comprehensive win over Hearts to end the season on a high-note.

Earlier in the competition, Rangers had scored a remarkable 27 goals as they cruised through to an Old Firm semi-final at Hampden, where goals from Chelsea Cornet and Kirsty Howat ensured victory over Celtic and a return to the national stadium for the final.

A stunning long-range effort from Rachel McLauchlan and a precision strike from Lizzie Arnot were enough to see off first-time finalists Hearts and allow Nicola Docherty to get her hands on the trophy as the first Rangers Women captain to lift the cup.

|  | HOME | RESULT | AWAY |
|---|---|---|---|
| R3 | Inverness | 0-12 | Rangers |
| R4 | Rangers | 9-0 | Dundee United |
| QF | Hibbernian | 2-6 | Rangers |
| SF | Rangers | 2-0 | Celtic |

# RANGERS WOMEN

Jo's playing career lasted more than 20 years, including three stints with Birmingham City plus time at eight other clubs. As well as her international caps, she also appeared in three FA Cup finals, winning with Birmingham in 2012. After leaving her role as Assistant Head coach at Birmingham, it did not take Potter long to begin working her magic at Rangers, implementing an effective recruitment strategy, a clearly defined playing style and delivering effective communication that ensured players, officials and supporters were all able to embrace her vision. By March 2024, Potter had steered Rangers on an unbeaten run of 22 games and was rewarded with a contract extension through season 2025/26. After winning two cups, Potter's Rangers fell just short of an historic treble in her first year but you can be sure she will be looking to go one step further before her contract concludes.

## FACT FILE

**NAME:**
Josanne Potter

**Date of Birth:**
13 November 1984

**Place of Birth:**
Mansfield, England

**England Caps:**
35 Including 2015 World Cup/2017 Euros

**Appointed Rangers Manager:**
22 June 2023

# RANGERS WOMEN
## STAR PLAYERS

### Kirsty Maclean

Despite missing several months of the season due to a knee injury, midfielder Kirsty Maclean was still named in the SWPL Team of the Year for season 2023/24 and was also voted as Players' Player of the Year by her Rangers team-mates. Solid rehabilitation helped Kirsty return in time to grab a Scottish Cup winner's medal and also bring her tally of Scotland caps up to 7 before the end of the season.

### Nicola Docherty

Nicola was appointed captain of Rangers Women in August 2023 and has since extended her contract by a further two years through to 2026. Now in the veteran category but still a current Scotland internationalist, Nicola brought a wealth of valuable experience from several seasons at Glasgow City and will be looking forward to raising further trophies as Rangers' skipper and adding to her extensive personal collection of medals and caps.

### Olivia McLoughlin

Liv joined Rangers on loan from Aston Villa during season 2023/24 and quickly became a fans' favourite during 20 appearances, including a goal in the Sky Sports Cup final. In June 2024, Rangers were delighted to secure her services on a two-year permanent deal and can look forward to her anchoring the midfield in the quest for further honours.

### Mia McAulay

Mia signed her first professional contract with Rangers in July 2023 at the age of 17 and immediately became one of the club's most recognisable, energetic and effective stars. In August 2023, Mia claimed the first ever SWPL Goal of the Month award with a shot from the far edge of the box against Aberdeen and went on to scoop the PFA Scotland Young Player of the Year award.

# RANGERS' BEST

# LEAGUE CUP MOMENTS

## No.2 2009/10

## THE DETAILS

| ST MIRREN 0 | RANGERS 1 |
|---|---|
| – | Miller 84 |
| Hampden Park 21st March 2010 | |

# WE ONLY NEED 9 MEN

## THE STORY

With Rangers down to nine men and extra-time only 6 minutes away, things were looking bleak for the Ibrox men before Kenny Miller popped up to head home a Steven Naismith cross and secure a seemingly unlikely win.

The Light Blues went into the game with confidence, in what would turn out to be a league-winning season. Neil Alexander retained his place in goal having deputised for Allan McGregor throughout the competition and his clean sheet, behind the experienced David Weir, proved vital in the end.

The Buddies had the better of the first half and gained a numerical advantage on 53 minutes when Kevin Thomson saw red for a lunge on his namesake, Steven Thomson. Things got worse 18 minutes later when young central defender Danny Wilson was also dismissed after his foul denied St Mirren forward Craig Dargo a clear goal-scoring opportunity.

In the 84th minute, Weir smothered another St Mirren attack and then drove forward to set up a short-handed breakaway. His pass released Naismith on the wing and the substitute's cross found Miller bursting into the box. The Musselburgh man's flicked header hit precisely the right spot to beat Paul Gallacher and crown an improbable and deliriously celebrated victory.

# WORDSEARCH

HIDDEN IN THE GRID BELOW ARE THE SURNAMES OF 9 MEN'S TEAM PLAYERS AND 4 WOMEN'S TEAM PLAYERS. CAN YOU FIND THEM ALL?

| O | G | W | K | S | A | R | N | T | G | O | Y | F | D |
|---|---|---|---|---|---|---|---|---|---|---|---|---|---|
| A | I | S | N | Y | U | T | F | E | J | L | C | J | O |
| I | D | I | O | M | A | N | D | E | S | I | O | H | C |
| N | O | S | N | I | K | L | I | W | D | N | R | H | H |
| A | C | T | S | D | N | B | U | T | L | A | N | D | E |
| D | H | E | N | I | F | I | D | A | D | D | K | A | R |
| B | E | R | I | O | L | N | K | A | C | S | G | L | D |
| J | R | L | K | M | T | A | B | S | T | M | L | T | S |
| E | T | I | L | A | C | A | A | E | A | J | D | U | I |
| F | Y | N | I | N | L | O | R | L | J | R | A | B | I |
| T | R | G | W | A | I | L | R | C | O | R | N | E | T |
| E | D | R | I | D | I | H | O | T | M | C | A | U | L |
| G | T | S | A | A | W | R | N | N | E | A | H | R | T |
| I | N | T | W | B | C | O | R | T | H | S | U | J | U |

WILKINSON    BUTLAND    RASKIN

DOCHERTY    BARRON    CORNET

DANILO    CORTES    JEFTE

NSIALA    STERLING

DIOMANDE    MCAULAY

SOLUTION ON PAGE 61.

# WORD GRID

Arrange the surnames of these current Rangers and Rangers Women players into the grid to reveal the name of a current Rangers forward

BUTLAND    NSIALA    MIDDAG
SOUTTAR    DIOMANDE    BALOGUN

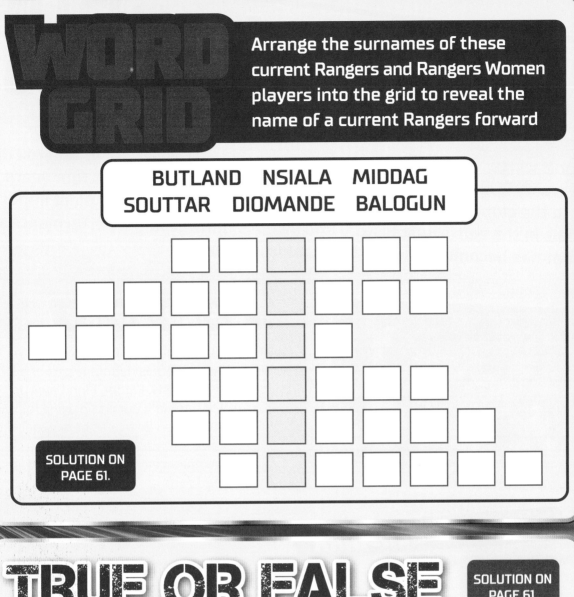

SOLUTION ON PAGE 61.

# TRUE OR FALSE

SOLUTION ON PAGE 61.

| | | TRUE | FALSE |
|---|---|---|---|
| 1 | Rangers are the only club to have won the league title at all 4 levels in current SPFL set-up | ☐ | ☐ |
| 2 | Ross County had never beaten Rangers in a competitive game before their comeback win on 14th April 2024 | ☐ | ☐ |
| 3 | The penalty awarded to Kilmarnock at Ibrox on 2nd January 2024 was the first conceded by Rangers in 75 league games | ☐ | ☐ |
| 4 | Rangers defeated Spartak Moscow 3-2 to win the 1972 European Cup Winners' Cup | ☐ | ☐ |
| 5 | Rangers Women have never won the Scottish Cup | ☐ | ☐ |
| 6 | Rangers Women play their home games at Dumbarton Football Stadium | ☐ | ☐ |

# BRIAN LAUDRUP SCRAPBOOK

Iconic winger Brian Laudrup was a very welcome return visitor to Ibrox in February 2024. The elegant Dane was a great favourite in his four years with the club and will be remembered for scoring one of the most important goals in the club's long history and also his unforgettable performance in what has become known as 'The Laudrup Final'.

## A STAR IS BORN

Brian was born on 22nd February 1969 in Vienna, Austria but is definitely part of a Danish footballing dynasty. Father, Finn Laudrup, won 19 caps for Denmark but was playing for Wiener SC in Vienna when Brian was born. Elder brother Michael also enjoyed a storied career as both player and manager, making 104 appearances for Denmark.

## PRINCE OF DENMARK

Brian went on to earn 82 caps and score 21 goals for his country. The undoubted highlight was Denmark's shock win at the 1992 European Championships in Sweden. Denmark had failed to qualify for the tournament and were only awarded a place ten days before the finals commenced due to the war in Yugoslavia. Their chances of winning were considered so low that Michael Laudrup declined to participate and so missed a chance to join brother Brian in lifting the trophy.

## SIGNING FOR RANGERS

Brian had already enjoyed success with Brondby, Bayer Uerdingen and Bayern Munich before he signed for Rangers from Fiorentina in July 1994 for a fee of around £2.3m. Laudrup signed on at Ibrox on the same day as Champions League winner Basile Boli of Marseille, but it would be the Danish man who prospered most in Glasgow.

## INSTANT SUCCESS

A stylish winger with elegance, pace and power, Brian enjoyed a very successful first season in light blue. 13 goals in 38 appearances helped the club retain the league title for a 7th successive time and he became the first overseas player to be named Scottish PFA Player of the Year.

## HAMPDEN HERO

In season 1995/96, Laudrup was joined by Paul Gascoigne and they propelled the team to further success, retaining the league title and adding the Scottish Cup. The 5-1 win over Hearts became known as 'The Laudrup Final' after an imperious performance from the Great Dane in which he scored twice and set up all three goals of Gordon Durie's hat-trick.

## NINE IN A ROW

In May 1997, a rare headed goal by Brian secured a 1-0 win for Rangers over Dundee United at Tannadice which clinched a historic 9th title in a row for the Ibrox club. In a wonderful team spearheaded by the likes of McCoist, Albertz, Gough and Gascoigne, it was again Laudrup who was elected Scottish PFA Player of the Year.

## AFTER RANGERS

After one more season, Laudrup left Rangers for brief stints with Chelsea and FC Copenhagen before winding up his career with Ajax. In 2004, Brian was named as one of FIFA's top 125 greatest living footballers.

## BACK AT IBROX

When Rangers welcomed FC Copenhagen to Govan for a friendly game on 16th January 2024, a still fresh-faced Brian Laudrup was in attendance to receive a very warm welcome from the Ibrox faithful. Having been elected to the Rangers Hall of Fame, his name will forever be honoured at Ibrox.

# PLAN B

The development of exceptional young talent is the main priority of the Rangers Academy, with several stars already making a contribution to the first team, including Cole McKinnon, Zak Lovelace and Bailey Rice last season.

## THE GRADUATE

Having joined the Rangers Academy in 2019, 21-year-old winger Ross McCausland made his big breakthrough last season with 39 first team appearances and 4 goals, earning the Men's Young Player of the Year award. The Co Antrim youngster also earned his first senior cap for Northern Ireland in November 2023 and will look to kick on again in 2024/25.

## BEST v BEST

After two seasons playing in the Scottish Lowland Football League, Rangers withdrew their B team from the competition after the club's proposal to introduce a revised Conference League was rejected.

The B Team continued to represent the club in the SPFL Trust Trophy, beating the first teams of The Spartans, Stenhousemuir and Alloa, before falling to Airdrie in the last 16.

Comprehensive wins over Queens Park and Partick Thistle also took them to the Glasgow Cup Final in February 2024, where they went down 3-0 to Celtic B.

The Rangers youngsters also gained high-level experience in a series of 'Best v Best' challenge matches against other top clubs' B teams and U21 sides, including Manchester City, Everton, Brentford, AS Monaco and Royal Antwerp.

# B TEAM GOAL OF THE SEASON

Rangers B defeated their Burnley counterparts 5-3 in an eventful challenge match in July 2023. Zak Lovelace notched 5 assists, while Bailey Rice picked up the B Team Goal of the Season award for his spectacular strike. Having already made his first team debut as a 16-year-old in 2022, Rice featured twice more in 2023/24 and also stepped up to the Scotland U19 team.

# SCOTTISH YOUTH CUP WINNERS

Rangers U18 side brought the Scottish FA Youth Cup back to Ibrox in April 2024 after defeating Aberdeen's U18 league-winning team 2-1 at Hampden Park. Findlay Curtis and Josh Gentles scored the goals but goalkeeper Mason Munn saved the day with a superb late stop. The tall 18-year-old Northern Irishman appears to have all the qualities to be a top-class keeper for club and country.

# ACADEMY PLAYER OF THE YEAR

21-year-old midfielder Cole McKinnon's performances earned him the Academy Player of the Year award and three substitute appearances for the first team, including away to Benfica in the Europa League.

WINNERS 2024

SCOTTISH FA
YOUTH CUP FINAL

# THE OTHER RANGERS

In October 2023, the popular Korean K-pop band STAY-C became a worldwide viral sensation after being photographed wearing crop-top versions of a vintage Rangers FC home shirt in Dallas, Texas. Unfortunately, they had got 'the wrong' Rangers as they had intended to honour the local Texas Rangers baseball team, who were then just days away from winning the World Series.

The girls, who earlier that year had scored a No. 1 single in South Korea with the song 'Teddy Bear', saw the funny side of the mix-up and even visited Ibrox a few months later for a photo-shoot.

## HOW MANY 'OTHER RANGERS' DO YOU KNOW?

Rangers is a popular name for football clubs, especially in Scotland, England and Northern Ireland, but there are also Rangers in at least 8 other countries around the world, including Hong Kong, Chile, Kenya and Nigeria. You can also find Rangers in rugby and other sports, including two household names in America who both proudly sport red, white and blue colours.

Here, we will take a look at some of them and also test your 'Other Rangers' knowledge.

## TEXAS RANGERS

Baseball's Texas Rangers take their name from the legendary law enforcement agency established in that state in 1835. They were crowned world champions after winning the World Series in 2023.

**QUESTION:** Texas Rangers' home ballpark is Globe Life Field in Arlington TX. Which NFL team plays in the adjacent AT&T Stadium?

## NEW YORK RANGERS

Founded in 1926, New York's Rangers were one of the 'Original Six' teams in ice hockey's National Hockey League and are four-time winners of the Stanley Cup.

**QUESTION:** Which legendary NYC multi-sport arena do the New York Rangers call home?

## QUEENS PARK RANGERS FC

West London's QPR were founded in 1882 as Christchurch Rangers. Their distinctive blue & white hooped shirts have regularly appeared at the top level of English football but the club has been stuck in the second-tier EFL Championship since 2015.

**QUESTION:** Former Rangers Head Coach Michael Beale moved to Ibrox from QPR in 2022. Which other former Rangers boss did he replace at Loftus Road earlier that year?

## BERWICK RANGERS FC

Berwick Rangers currently play in the Lowland League, but before relegation in 2019 they were the only English team to play in the Scottish Professional Football League set-up.

Under player / manager Jock Wallace, 'The Wee Gers' achieved a famous 1-0 Scottish Cup victory over Rangers in January 1967.

**QUESTION:**

Berwick-upon-Tweed's Shielfield Park is home to Berwick Rangers FC and which other professional sports team?

## THE LONE RANGER

The fictional masked crime-fighter is a legendary figure from vintage TV Westerns. The courageous former Texas Ranger is best remembered for his "Hi-Ho Silver" catchphrase and his Native American side-kick Tonto.

**QUESTION:** Which Rangers striker scored a late winner against Hearts at Ibrox in October 2023 while wearing a Lone Ranger-style mask to protect an injury?

# THE GOALIES

Only a handful of goal-keepers have consistently proved that they can handle the high expectations and extreme pressure of being Rangers No. 1. Remarkably, in the last 90 years or so at Ibrox, the gloves have passed almost seamlessly between just nine men in an astonishing display of excellence and longevity.

## JAMES 'JERRY' DAWSON (1929-1946)

'The Prince of Goalkeepers' was first choice keeper from 1932/33 onwards, winning 5 league titles before the outbreak of war. Jerry continued to serve club and country throughout the war, adding 6 wartime regional league medals and appearing in 9 wartime internationals.

## BOBBY BROWN (1946-1956)

Remarkably, Brown maintained a distinguished career in teaching at the same time as playing top-level football on a part-time basis. Playing behind the legendary 'Iron Curtain' defence, he appeared in 179 consecutive league matches between August 1946 and April 1952, including the first ever Scottish domestic treble in season 1948/49.

## GEORGE NIVEN (1951-1962)

Fifer 'Wee George' is remembered as one of the bravest stoppers to wear the yellow jersey. Despite a calamitous 7-1 defeat to Celtic in 1957, Niven recovered to be ever-present in the title-winning side of 1958/59 and won a 5th League-winner's medal in 1960/61 before leaving for Partick Thistle.

## PETER McCLOY (1970-1986)

Affectionately known as 'The Girvan Lighthouse', McCloy was an ever-present for 'The Barca Bears' team which won the 1972 Cup Winners' Cup Final in Spain. Having first been selected by Willie Waddell, McCloy amassed over 500 appearances for the club and was still registered as a player in 1986/87 while coaching under Graeme Souness.

## BILLY RITCHIE (1955-1967)

Billy Ritchie debuted for Rangers in 1956, before his career was interrupted by National Service. After regaining the gloves, he excelled as Rangers reached a European final in 1960/61 and anchored the domestic treble winning team in 1963/64.

*Norrie Martin, Erik Sorensen and Gerry Neef were Rangers' most prominent goalkeepers in the latter half of the 1960s, with Martin selected for the 1967 European Cup Winners' Cup Final against Bayern Munich.*

*McCloy was second-choice behind Stewart Kennedy and Jim Stewart at times but always outlasted his replacements before finally being displaced by Nicky Walker.*

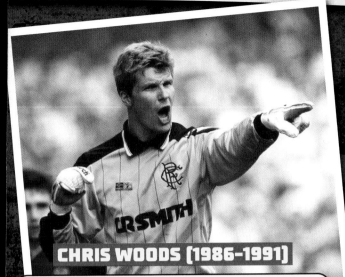

## CHRIS WOODS (1986-1991)

An England international, Woods played 230 games for Rangers and claimed a clean sheet in more than half of them, as the club claimed several major honours during his tenure. In October 1987, Woods was red-carded, arrested and ultimately convicted for his actions in an explosive Old Firm derby. The implementation of a controversial 'three foreigners' rule in 1991 saw him return to English domestic football.

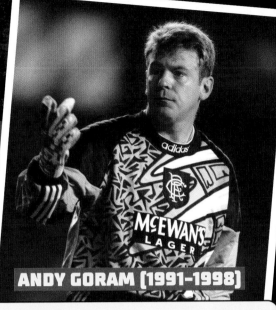

## ANDY GORAM (1991-1998)

Known simply as 'The Goalie', Goram's dominance against Celtic in particular became legendary. In his 26 Old Firm games, 'The Goalie' only conceded 22 goals and his record of 15 wins and 6 draws helped the club secure 6 titles during his time.

## STEFAN KLOS (1998-2007)

Replacing Goram, 'Der Goalie' was also a brilliant shot-stopper and excelled in the big games. He played in all 48 games of the domestic treble in 2002/03 and was later made club captain. A knee injury in January 2005 effectively ended his first-team career, but Klos did make a final European appearance in March 2007.

*Klos was initially replaced by a young Allan McGregor, and then by Ronald Waterreus and Lionel Letizi before 'Greegsy' made the job his own.*

## ALLAN McGREGOR (2002-2012 & 2018-2023)

Signed as a youth in 1998, McGregor finally broke through as first choice in 2006/07, claiming 3 league titles and the first of 42 Scotland caps before his first spell was broken by the club's liquidation. He returned in 2018 and helped clinch the club's 55th title in 2020/21. Allan also played in the 2022 Europa League Final, having missed out on the UEFA Cup final in 2008 due to injury. 25 years after first signing, McGregor retired at the age of 41, having made over 500 appearances for the club.

*Neil Alexander, Cammy Bell and Steve Simonsen all played a part in the journey back from the lower leagues. Wes Foderingham took over in 2015/16 before McGregor reclaimed the gloves in 2018.*

# RANGERS' BEST

# LEAGUE CUP MOMENTS

## No.3 1996/97

## THE DETAILS

| RANGERS 4 | HEARTS 3 |
|---|---|
| McCoist 11, 27; Gascoigne 64, 66 | Fulton 44, Robertson 59, Weir 88 |
| Celtic Park 24th November 1996 ||

# E GREATEST LEAGUE CUP FINAL EVER?

## THE STORY

In a retrospective article in 2016, The Scotsman newspaper suggested that this might have been the greatest League Cup Final ever, but it nearly didn't take place at all. As Hampden was unavailable, the game was moved to Celtic Park but with the East End of Glasgow in the grip of a blizzard, the match was only confirmed one hour before kick-off.

Rangers got off to a hot start when imperious winger Brian Laudrup sliced through the Hearts defence to set up McCoist's opener in 11 minutes. The Scotland striker added a second shortly after that with his record-equalling 50th goal in the competition. Hearts got one back before the interval and when John Robertson netted on the hour mark it was game-on. Spurred into action after a half-time dressing room bust up, Paul Gascoigne then stepped up and took a grip of the game, surging forward to snatch two goals in three minutes and, despite a late Hearts goal through future Ranger Davie Weir, that was enough to win the cup.

Even Hearts Fans remember this game with some pride but it is the dramatic nature of Rangers' victory and the beaming smiles of Gazza and Super Ally celebrating on the Parkhead pitch which will live longest in the memory.

# SPOT THE BALL

Use your skill and judgement to find the real ball. Answers on page 61.

# WHAT'S MY NAME?

Use the clues provided to reorder the letters in red to find the players' real names.

| | |
|---|---|
| | ALAN ASK HIS OAF – Zambian intl. now playing in Saudi Pro League |
| | DONUTS JINGLER – Versatile Englishman |
| | NANCI STALLION – defender, formerly of AC Milan |
| | CLAM LOG RANGER – legendary goalkeeper |
| | ADD SHAVEN THREEPENNY – Assistant Manager |
| | CLAIM GHOUL VIOLIN – Ex-Aston Villa Women |
| | JET TROOP – Women Manager |
| | AIRLOCK NISSAN – Belgian midfielder |
| | BALD JACK NUT – Goalkeeper |
| | CHOSEN TREACLE – Scotland international Women |
| | ARCTIC DONE HOLY – Women's captain |
| | ABLE LOG NOUN – Nigerian defender |

SOLUTIONS ON PAGE 61.

# WALTER SMITH
## A MONUMENTAL RANGERS ICON

"Walter wasn't just the greatest manager of the modern era; he was the finest of human beings. He was a man of supremely strong character and was also kind, thoughtful and generous."
*John Bennett, Chairman, Rangers FC, 25th May 2024*

Walter Smith OBE first came to Ibrox as a boyhood supporter. He went on to manage the club, bringing 10 league titles and a legacy of success to Govan over two spells as manager.

In May 2024, the club unveiled a statue of the great man in the shadow of the Copland Road Stand which replaced the East Terrace from where the young Walter watched and dreamt of glory.

The statue was created in bronze by renowned royal sculptor Douglas Jennings and sits atop a marble plinth inscribed with Smith's record as both manager and assistant.

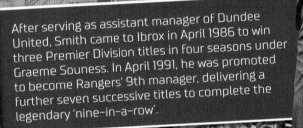

After serving as assistant manager of Dundee United, Smith came to Ibrox in April 1986 to win three Premier Division titles in four seasons under Graeme Souness. In April 1991, he was promoted to become Rangers' 9th manager, delivering a further seven successive titles to complete the legendary 'nine-in-a-row'.

Smith's second spell as boss ended after clinching the club's 54th title in the final league game of season 2010/11. He remained an influential and respected figure at Ibrox after retirement before his death in October 2021.

As well as his many club honours, Walter Smith received an honorary doctorate from Glasgow Caledonian University in 2012 in recognition of his football achievements. He was made an Officer of the Order of the British Empire in 1997.

WALTER SMITH O.B.E
1948 - 2021

# 'SUPER' ALLY McCOIST OBE

As well as being one of the most popular former Rangers players of all time, Ally McCoist also has a host of admirers outside of Ibrox too, gaining popularity around the country and beyond through his TV and radio work. Even The King is apparently a fan; Ally was awarded an OBE in the June 2024 honours list.

## EARLY CAREER

Born in Bellshill in 1962, McCoist made his professional debut for St Johnstone in 1979. His prolific goal-scoring earned him a £400,00 move to Sunderland in 1981, although he was less successful on Wearside.

## RANGERS

John Greig brought McCoist to Rangers for a fee of £185,000 in 1983. By the time he played his last game for the club 15 years later, Coisty had scored 355 goals in competitive fixtures, including 23 hat-tricks, while contributing to 10 Premier League wins and 9 League Cups, although surprisingly, he only claimed 1 Scottish Cup winner's medal in light blue.

Ally retired from playing in 2001 after 3 seasons with Kilmarnock.

## SCOTLAND

McCoist won 61 caps and scored 19 goals for Scotland, despite breaking a leg against Portugal in 1993. Coisty's most memorable international strike was the only goal of the game against Switzerland at Villa Park in Euro 96.

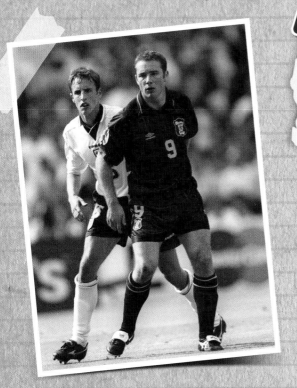

## IN THE DUGOUT

In 2007, Ally came back into the game as assistant manager to his old gaffer Walter Smith at Ibrox. He succeeded Smith to become the 13th manager of Rangers in 2011, playing a vital role in starting the climb back up the leagues after the events of 2012, before handing in his notice in December 2014.

## TV AND FILM

Ally's lovable cheeky-chappie personality made him a natural for a career in broadcasting.

He made 363 appearances as a team captain on the BBC's A Question of Sport from 1996 to 2007, alongside host Sue Barker and rival captains John Parrott, Frankie Dettori and Matt Dawson. Ally even confessed to sometimes writing a cheat sheet on his arm to help get the upper hand.

He also co-presented the late-night Scottish TV chat show 'McCoist and MacAulay' in the 1990s and even starred in Robert Duvall's movie 'A Shot at Glory' as fictional ex-Celtic player Jackie McQuillan.

## PUNDIT

Ally was featured as a commentator on EA Sports' popular video game series 'FIFA' from 1998 to 2005.

In real life, he is a popular pundit and co-commentator on TV, appearing on ITV, BT Sport, Sky and Amazon. His knowledge and enthusiasm have made him a viewers' favourite and he has been known to reference his love of rock music in broadcasts, particularly AC/DC.

## RADIO

Ally's cheeky face is not exactly one made for radio, but he has also found a home presenting on talkSPORT alongside Jeff Stelling, Laura Woods and Alan Brazil, among others.

## RANGERS' BEST

# LEAGUE CUP MOMENTS

## No.4 1993/94

**SU**
**SU**

## THE DETAILS

| RANGERS 2 | HIBERNIAN 1 |
|---|---|
| Durrant 55, McCoist 81 | McPherson OG 59 |
| Celtic Park 24th October 1993 | |

# PER ALLY: PER SUB

## THE STORY

With Hampden under redevelopment, Rangers hosted Celtic in the semi-final at Ibrox after winning a coin toss to determine home advantage. They squeezed through with the only goal of the game from Mark Hateley to set up a final with Hibs at Celtic Park. Hateley started up front alongside Ian Durrant in the final and it was their one-two passing move that set the Scotsman up to chip over Jim Leighton and give Rangers the lead early in the second half. Dave McPherson threw Hibs a lifeline shortly after that with a clumsy own goal but Walter Smith still had a trump card in reserve. Ally McCoist had been out of the picture after breaking a leg in Portugal on Scotland duty earlier in the year but he stepped off the bench to win the game with a spectacular overhead kick in a fairy-tale finish.

51

# A LOOK BA

2024/25 will be another important season for Rangers as they look to add more treasures to the incredible Trophy Room at Ibrox and retain their proud record as the club with the most Scottish League Championships to their name.

Here, we look back in time at how Rangers fared in some corresponding milestone seasons over the last 100 years.

## 10 Years Ago

### 2014/15 – A Cautionary Tale

Definitely a season to forget for Rangers as chaos reigned on and off the park. This should have been the season when the club completed a smooth return to the top league after liquidation, but ownership wrangling, legal trouble and financial woes undermined their chances on the pitch. Working under 3 different Chairmen and 3 different Managers, the first team won only 19 of their 36 games in the Championship, finishing third behind champions Hearts and Hibs. That was still good enough to reach the promotion play-offs, but a 6-1 aggregate thumping by Motherwell meant that the club had to wait one more year to finish the job.

## 20 Years Ago

### 2004/05 – Helicopter Sunday

With Alex McLeish at the helm, Rangers claimed their 51st League title on a dramatic final day in May 2005. Celtic went to Fir Park two points clear at the top and scored first, but two late goals from Motherwell's Scott McDonald snatched the points away from them. As a result, top scorer Nacho Novo's only-goal winner at Hibs was enough to clinch the crown for Rangers and divert the SPFL helicopter and the trophy to Easter Road. Rangers had earlier won the League Cup with a 5-1 win over Motherwell. The assertive Dutchman, Fernando Ricksen, appeared in all 51 competitive games and was selected as PFA Scotland Player of the Year (joint with John Hartson).

## 50 Years Ago

### 1974/75 – Rangers Block Celtic's Ten-in-a-Row Quest

Before the introduction of the Scottish Premier Division, Rangers won the last-ever Scottish Football League Division One title in 1975, finishing seven points clear of Hibs and ending third-placed Celtic's run of consecutive titles at nine. There was to be no cup success though. Rangers failed to progress from their League Cup group, lost to Aberdeen in the Scottish Cup, Celtic in the Drybrough Cup and, in a season where the Gers did not compete in Europe, they were defeated by Southampton in the Texaco Cup. Derek Parlane finished top goal scorer with 18, two more than Derek Johnstone, while Stewart Kennedy and Sandy Jardine were ever-presents, with the latter being elected as Footballer of the Year in Scotland.

## 100 Years Ago

### 1924/25 – 3-in-a-row with "The Wee Blue Devil"

Rangers claimed their 3rd consecutive League title in 1924/25, their 4th title under Bill Struth and 13th overall, finishing 3 points clear of Airdrieonians. The side was captained by Tommy Cairns and included future Hall of Famers Davie Meiklejohn and Sandy Archibald, who would go on to make a record 513 league appearances for the club, while Geordie Henderson was the club's top scorer for the 4th season in a row. The undoubted star of the show however, was the diminutive winger, Alan Morton, later to earn the 'Wee Blue Devil' nickname while starring for Scotland's 'Wembley Wizards' in 1928. Morton was Struth's first-ever signing in 1920 and, after a remarkable career in which he combined his profession as a mining engineer with part-time football, his portrait hangs at the top of the famous marble staircase in the main stand at Ibrox as a testament to his genius.

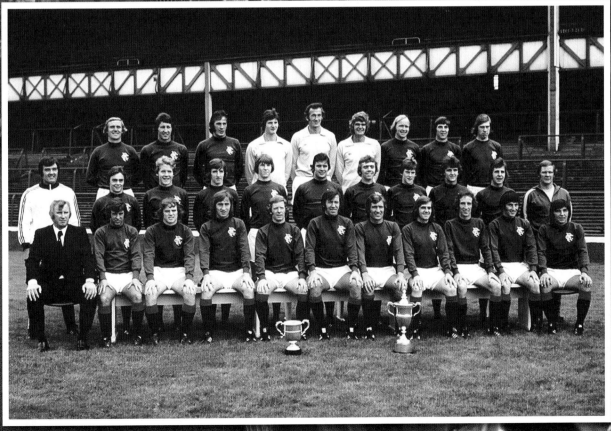

# PLAYER PROFILES

## OSCAR CORTES

| | |
|---|---|
| **DoB** | 3 December 2003 |
| **Country** | Colombia |
| **Position** | Winger |
| **Previous Club** | RC Lens (France) |

Oscar Cortes officially began his second loan spell at Rangers in June 2024, but this time it came with an obligation to buy and a four-year contract. The young winger initially came on loan from RC Lens in January 2024 but suffered a severe muscle injury after just 7 games. Fortunately, Rangers had seen enough of his talent to confirm their interest and tie him up to a long-term deal. although injury struck again at Tynecastle in this season's opening game.

## CLINTON NSIALA – MAKENGO

| | |
|---|---|
| **DoB** | 17 January 2004 |
| **Country** | France |
| **Position** | Centre Back |
| **Previous Club** | AC Milan |

Ambitious Frenchman Nsiala spurned a contract extension at AC Milan in order to pursue his development at Ibrox. The left-footed defender gained valuable experience in his three years with I Rossoneri, performing strongly for their U19 team both domestically and in the UEFA Youth League, although he did not make an appearance for the first team, despite being named in several match day squads.

# JEFTE

| | |
|---|---|
| **DoB** | 21 December 2003 |
| **Country** | Brazil |
| **Position** | Left Back |
| **Previous Club** | Fluminense (Brazil) |

Jefte Vital da Silva Dias was born in Rio de Janeiro and will be expected to bring some Brazilian flair to Rangers' left flank after finally completing a transfer to Govan in May 2024. Rangers had hoped to complete the deal with Fluminense in the January 2024 transfer window but the terms of his one-year loan deal with Cypriot side APOEL complicated the situation. The highly rated 20-year-old is very quick with an appetite for goals, so, with a contract now in place until 2028, he is well-placed to make an impact at left back.

# LIAM KELLY

| | |
|---|---|
| **DoB** | 23 January 1996 |
| **Country** | Scotland |
| **Position** | Goalkeeper |
| **Previous Club** | Motherwell (Scotland) |

Glaswegian Kelly first signed for Rangers as a 10-year-old boy, but left in 2018 without playing a first team game for the club. Since then, he has racked up over 270 appearances for East Fife, Livingston, QPR and Motherwell. Kelly was appointed club captain at Fir Park and also made his international debut for Scotland in October 2023 as a Steelman. He was included in Scotland's squad for Euro 2024, having formally agreed terms to re-sign for Rangers after the tournament on a two-year deal.

# HAMZA IGAMANE

| | |
|---|---|
| **DoB** | 2 November 2002 |
| **Country** | Morocco |
| **Position** | Forward |
| **Previous Club** | AS FAR Rabat |

The young Moroccan striker arrived at Ibrox in July 2024 on a five-year deal, which should give the youngster, already capped eight times for his country at U23 level, plenty of time to fulfil his undoubted potential.

# CONNOR BARRON

**DoB** 29 August 2002
**Country** Scotland
**Position** Midfielder
**Previous Club** Aberdeen

Kintore-born midfielder Barron, a Scotland U21 internationalist, made the switch to Ibrox after the expiry of his Aberdeen contract. The former Dons youth player had already made over 100 first team appearances during his time with the Pittodrie club, including loan spells at Brechin City and Kelty Hearts.

# LEAH EDDIE

**DoB** 23 January 2001
**Country** Scotland
**Position** Centre Back
**Previous Club** Hibernian

Rangers Women were delighted to snap up Hibs' Player of the Year on a free transfer after the expiry of the Falkirk girl's contract in Leith. Leah had a very short stint with Rangers in 2018 but now returns as an established SWPL player and a full internationalist with Scotland.

# LAURA RAFFERTY

**DoB** 29 April 1996
**Country** Northern Ireland
**Position** Defender
**Previous Club** Southampton

The Southampton-born defender was a popular figure at her home-town club before making the switch to Glasgow on a two-year deal. Having previously played for Chelsea, Brighton and Bristol City, Laura has won over 30 caps for Northern Ireland and has also captained her country.

# KATIE WILKINSON

**DoB** 5 November 1994
**Country** England
**Position** Forward
**Previous Club** Southampton

Katie was Jo Potter's second capture from Southampton in the summer. The experienced striker was The Saints top scorer and Player of the Year last term and was also nominated for the English Women's Championship Player of the Season award. Katie's Rangers career got off to a great start with four goals in her first competitive game, at Aberdeen in August 2024.

# ROBIN PROPPER

**DoB** 23 September 1993
**Country** Netherlands
**Position** Centre Back
**Previous Club** FC Twente

Rangers were delighted to capture the tall defender by activating a release clause in his contract with FC Twente. The younger brother of former Brighton star Davy Propper, Robin had already played with another Ibrox newbie Vaclav Cerny in Enschede and had previously lined up alongside Cyriel Dessers at Heracles.

# VACLAV CERNY

**DoB** 17 October 1997
**Country** Czech Republic
**Position** Winger
**Previous Club** Wolfsburg

After appearing for his country against Georgia at Euro 2024, former Ajax youth prospect Cerny made the switch to Rangers on loan from Bundesliga side VfL Wolfsburg, having also previously starred at FC Twente and Utrecht. Cerny showed an early eye for goal with a stunner against Motherwell in the first game of the club's tenancy at Hampden, In August 2024.

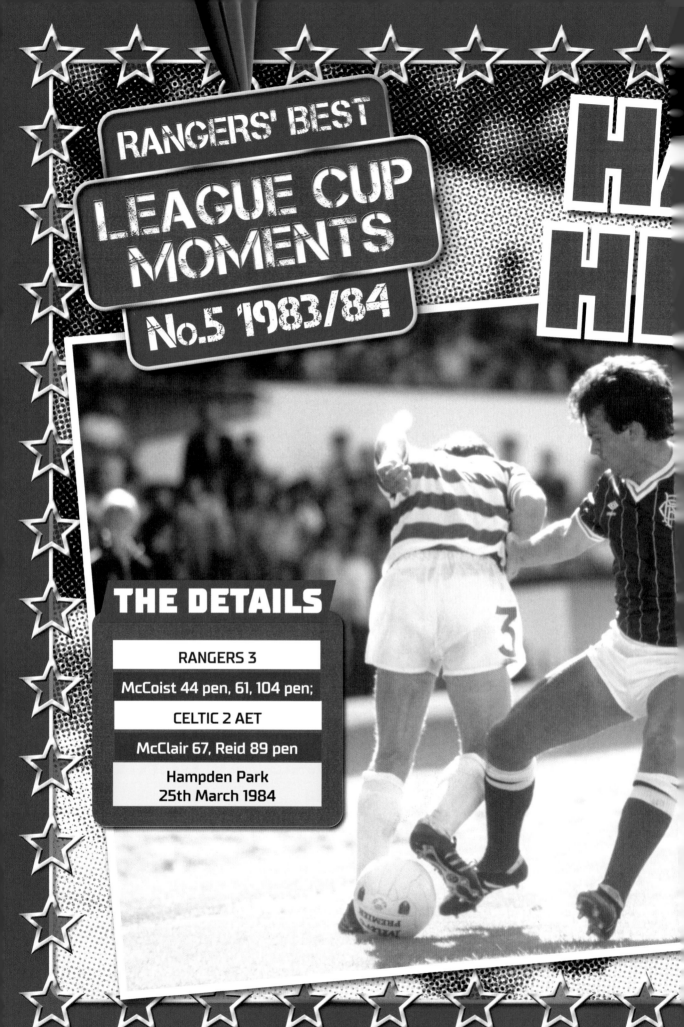

# RANGERS' BEST

# LEAGUE CUP MOMENTS

## No.5 1983/84

H
H
H

## THE DETAILS

| RANGERS 3 |
| --- |
| McCoist 44 pen, 61, 104 pen; |
| CELTIC 2 AET |
| McClair 67, Reid 89 pen |
| Hampden Park 25th March 1984 |

# T TRICK RO ALLY

## THE STORY

Rangers' path to the final saw them win all of their games in a group containing Hearts, Clydebank and St Mirren, before despatching Dundee United in a two-legged semi-final. That put them on a collision course with Celtic at Hampden Park in a ferociously contested final that saw three penalties, eight bookings and the emergence of a hat-trick hero.

Late in the first half, Bobby Russell, playing one of his finest games in blue, won a penalty which was slotted home by Ally McCoist and the wee striker added his second after the interval from close range. Brian McClair pulled one back before McCoist was again involved in penalty action at the very end of the game, only this time it was his foul which conceded a spot kick from which Mark Reid sent the game into extra time.

Roared on by Jock Wallace in his second spell as manager, Rangers pushed forward and inevitably McCoist was involved in further penalty drama. After a foul on him by Roy Aitken, McCoist's second penalty of the day was initially saved by Bonner, but he was alert enough to net the rebound, securing the cup for his team and establishing himself as a Rangers' goal-scoring legend.

# COLOURING IN

Come on all you artists out there! Use your skills and your colour pencils to see if you can recreate the look of the inset picture.

# ANSWERS

## P24 SPOT THE DIFFERENCE

## P25 WHO AM I?

CYRIEL DESSERS

## P34 WORDSEARCH

| O | G | W | K | S | A | R | N | T | G | O | Y | F | D |
|---|---|---|---|---|---|---|---|---|---|---|---|---|---|
| A | I | S | N | Y | U | T | F | E | J | L | C | J | O |
| I | O | I | O | M | A | N | D | E | S | I | O | H | C |
| N | O | S | N | I | K | L | I | W | D | N | R | H | H |
| A | C | T | S | D | N | B | U | T | L | A | N | D | E |
| D | H | E | N | I | F | I | D | A | D | O | K | A | R |
| B | E | R | I | O | L | N | K | A | C | S | G | L | D |
| J | R | L | K | M | T | A | B | S | T | M | L | T | S |
| E | T | I | L | A | C | A | A | E | A | J | D | U | I |
| F | Y | N | I | N | L | O | R | L | J | R | A | B | I |
| T | R | G | W | A | I | L | R | C | O | R | N | E | T |
| E | D | R | I | D | I | H | O | T | M | C | A | U | L |
| G | T | S | A | A | W | R | N | N | E | A | H | R | T |
| I | N | T | W | B | C | O | R | T | H | S | U | J | U |

## P35 WORD GRID

```
    M I   D D A G
  D I O M A N D E
B U T L A N D
    N S I A L A
    B A L O G U N
    S O U T T A R
```

## P35 TRUE OR FALSE

1. TRUE
2. TRUE
3. TRUE
4. FALSE It was Dynamo Moscow
5. FALSE They won it in 2024
6. FALSE Broadwood Stadium, Cumbernauld

## P40-41 OTHER RANGERS

Texas Rangers = Dallas Cowboys
New York Rangers = Madison Square Garden
QPR = Mark Warburton
Berwick Rangers = Berwick Bandits Speedway team
Lone Ranger = Danilo

## P46 SPOT THE BALL

## P46 WHAT'S MY NAME?

ALAN ASK HIS OAF – Fashion Sakala
DONUTS JINGLER – Dujon Sterling
NANCI STALLION – Clinton Nsiala
CLAM LOG RANGER – Allan McGregor
ADD SHAVEN THREEPENNY – Stephan Van Der Heyden
CLAIM GHOUL VIOLIN – Olivia McLoughlin
JET TROOP – Jo Potter
AIRLOCK NISSAN – Nicolas Raskin
BALD JACK NUT – Jack Butland
CHOSEN TREACLE – Chelsea Cornet
ARCTIC DONE HOLY – Nicola Docherty
ABLE LOG NOUN – Leon Balogun

# ROLL OF HONOUR

**EUROPEAN CUP WINNERS' CUP**

1971-72

**SCOTTISH PREMIERSHIP**

1890-91, 1898-99, 1899-1900, 1900-01, 1901-02, 1910-11, 1911-12, 1912-13, 1917-18, 1919-20, 1920-21, 1922-23, 1923-24, 1924-25, 1926-27, 1927-28, 1928-29, 1929-30, 1930-31, 1932-33, 1933-34, 1934-35, 1936-37, 1938-39, 1946-47, 1948-49, 1949-50, 1952-53, 1955-56, 1956-57, 1958-59, 1960-61, 1962-63, 1963-64, 1974-75, 1975-76, 1977-78, 1986-87, 1988-89, 1989-90, 1990-91, 1991-92, 1992-93, 1993-94, 1994-95, 1995-96, 1996-97, 1998-99, 1999-2000, 2002-03, 2004-05, 2008-09, 2009-10, 2010-11, 2020-21

**SCOTTISH CHAMPIONSHIP**

2015-16

**SCOTTISH LEAGUE ONE**

2013-14

**SCOTTISH LEAGUE TWO**

2012-13

**SCOTTISH CUP**

1893-94, 1896-97, 1897-98, 1902-03, 1927-28, 1929-30, 1931-32, 1933-34, 1934-35, 1935-36, 1947-48, 1948-49, 1949-50, 1952-53, 1959-60, 1961-62, 1962-63, 1963-64, 1965-66, 1972-73, 1975-76, 1977-78, 1978-79, 1980-81, 1991-92, 1992-93, 1995-96, 1998-99, 1999-2000, 2001-02, 2002-03, 2007-08, 2008-09, 2021-22

**SCOTTISH LEAGUE CUP**

1946-47, 1948-49, 1960-61, 1961-62, 1963-64, 1964-65, 1970-71, 1975-76, 1977-78, 1978-79, 1981-82, 1983-84, 1984-85, 1986-87, 1987-88, 1988-89, 1990-91, 1992-93, 1993-94, 1996-97, 1998-99, 2001-02, 2002-03, 2004-05, 2007-08, 2009-10, 2010-11, 2023-24

**SCOTTISH CHALLENGE CUP**

2015-16

**EMERGENCY WAR LEAGUE**

1939-40

**EMERGENCY WAR CUP**

1939-40

**SOUTHERN LEAGUE**

1940-41, 1941-42, 1942-43, 1943-44, 1944-45, 1945-46

**SOUTHERN LEAGUE CUP**

1940-41, 1941-42, 1942-43, 1944-45

**GLASGOW LEAGUE**

1895-96, 1897-98

**GLASGOW CUP**

1893, 1894, 1897, 1898, 1900, 1901, 1902, 1911, 1912, 1913, 1914, 1918, 1919, 1922, 1923, 1924, 1925, 1930, 1932, 1933, 1934, 1936, 1937, 1938, 1940, 1942, 1943, 1944, 1945, 1948, 1950, 1954, 1957, 1958, 1960, 1969, 1971, 1975 (shared), 1976, 1979, 1983, 1985, 1986, 1987

**VICTORY CUP**

1946

**SUMMER CUP**

1942

**GLASGOW MERCHANTS CHARITY CUP**

1878-79, 1896-97, 1899-1900, 1903-04, 1905-06, 1906-07, 1908-09, 1910-11, 1918-19, 1921-22, 1922-23, 1924-25, 1927-28, 1928-29, 1929-30, 1930-31, 1931-32, 1932-33, 1933-34, 1938-39, 1939-40, 1940-41, 1941-42, 1943-44, 1944-45, 1945-46, 1946-47, 1947-48, 1950-51, 1954-55, 1956-57, 1959-60